Tales o

Tales of Talent

A Modern Fable For Today's Leaders

How To Harness Your People's Talent
To Achieve Your Organisation's Vision

Guy Ellis

Illustrations by Caroline Evans

First Published In Great Britain 2006
by www.BookShaker.com

© Copyright Guy Ellis

All rights reserved. No part of this publication may be reproduced, stored in or introduced into a retrieval system, or transmitted, in any form, or by any means (electronic, mechanical, photocopying recording or otherwise) without the prior written permission of the publisher.

This book is sold subject to the condition that it shall not, by way of trade or otherwise, be lent, resold, hired out, or otherwise circulated without the publishers prior consent in any form of binding or cover other than that in which it is published and without a similar condition including this condition being imposed on the subsequent purchaser.

Typeset in Georgia

Dedicated to Ali, Kara and Cam – the other three initials that are Gack Consulting.

Acknowledgements

I would like to thank the many individuals from various organisations who allowed me to interview them as part of this book. Although the style, format and approach became very different to what I initially envisioned, without their input, I would not have had the confidence or passion to persevere. Those individuals were Helen Aldridge and Christine Cole (Prudential UK), Stephen Burke and David Leithead (Michael Page UK), Tom Crawford (Bernard Hodes on GSK), Melanie Gilbey (Walt Disney), Mike Gostick (Rabobank UK), Katrina Hale and Ross Vincent (Best International), Kevin Hogarth (Capital One), Tim Hurst (HB Solutions), Charles Morgan (AKS), Dave Thomas (Standard Chartered Bank), Andrew Thompson (Oxfam), Ralph Tribe (Getty Images) and Ian Williamson (BP).

A number of other people were important influences with either technical and/or emotional support, namely Caroline Burr, Sue Cuff, John Evans, Richard Griffiths, Gary Haslam, Chris O'Brien, Dominique Stafford, Stephanie Staton, Sally Talbot and Jackie Wearn. Thank you all.

I'd also like to thank Geraldine Kaye at GAAPs who first suggested the idea of writing this book.

Finally, my greatest thanks go to Catherine Heritage. Without her assistance, patience and honesty, this book would never have been completed.

Contents

ACKNOWLEDGEMENTS
CONTENTS
PREFACE

THE QUEEN'S VIEW 1
THE LORD CHAMBERLAIN'S VIEW 5
   THE PRESENTATION 10
THE KEEPER OF THE PRIVY PURSE'S VIEW 21
   THE LEGACY 26
      The Opportunity 26
      The Crisis – Part One 28
      The Crisis – Part Two 30
      The Repositioning 31
      The Opportunity Revisited 34
THE MASTER OF THE HOUSEHOLD'S VIEW 37
   THE ONE SIDED CONVERSATION 41
THE STEWARD'S VIEW 49
   THE MAN 53

Building The Vision *53*
Making The Vision Reality *54*
The Vision Stagnates *56*
...And Topples *57*
The New Day Comes? *60*
THE ROYAL VALET'S VIEW **65**
  THE MEETING 68
The Issue *68*
Delivering The Role *73*
Learning To Accept Help *75*
The Need For Consistent Reinforcement *78*
The Importance of Communication *80*
Bringing It All Together *81*
THE BOY'S VIEW **85**
THE QUEEN'S SPEECH **93**
EPILOGUE: SOME YEARS LATER **103**

ABOUT THE AUTHOR
ABOUT THE ILLUSTRATOR

Preface

My personal vision of organisations in the future...

There came a time when all organisations recognised that their employees were the only real variable in achieving long-term success;

where employees were recognised for inspiring others to feats greater than the sum of their individual parts;

where a unifying culture was seen as a way of holding a company together through the hard times and keeping it disciplined through the good;

where the good name of an organisation rested not on the latest TV advertisement but on the small, everyday actions of all employees and external partners, working towards the same goals;

and where it wasn't the big ideas of management that bought success but rather their ability to communicate and motivate employees to put them into action.

That time was not now.

But that time was coming.

This book invites you the reader, through the power of story telling, to identify with the characters you find in its pages and use this opportunity to reflect on your own experiences.

I believe that reflection is one of the most powerful ways we can learn. If you apply a few basic organisational tenets, which I outline in the last chapter, with events and feelings you have experienced firsthand, I believe that you will find the insights you seek.

This book does not assume that insight leads to easy answers. In fact, what I hope you take from this book is that unlike fairy tales, reality is not packaged in tidy chunks and doesn't often have neat endings. However, answers and the means to implement them are often closer than you think.

I have based this book on one principle – a principle so obvious that it is frequently forgotten, pushed aside or downplayed in the frantic search for deeper enlightenment. That principle is:

> **"Organisations are simply a group of people with shared interests or purpose."**

May I wish you thoughtful reading.

The Queen's View

The Queen looked out from her balcony across her kingdom and smiled, for there was much good throughout the land. Her realm was growing, her enemies were subdued and the gods were satisfied with her offerings.

She turned, noting as she did that a small boy was watching her. Looking over her shoulder, she asked his name.

"Janus," he said. "My name is Janus."

Turning back to face the boy, she asked him why he was watching her.

"I want to be a king when I grow older and a king has to rule wisely," he said. "But no one knows how I can learn to be wise. Some suggested that I watched you to learn. So here I am."

With a smile, the Queen asked the boy what he had learnt so far.

"Nothing yet," Janus responded, *"but I have plenty of time. You have been my Queen for as long as I can remember."*

As the Queen walked away, she noticed a storm brewing in the west. "Yet another challenge," she thought. As she slipped into her chambers, she quietly murmured, "and when will any of us have the time to teach the young?"

The Lord Chamberlain's View

The Lord Chamberlain heard the Queen re-enter the chambers. "Dreaming again," he mused. "Fine enough for her, but it doesn't get the crops gathered and sent to market."

As he settled down to his work again there was a commotion at the door and suddenly a Royal Valet burst in with a letter. "Sir," he panted, "I have important news from the fields."

The Lord Chamberlain grabbed the letter from the Royal Valet and began to read. "Dear Sir ... sorry to inform you ... unrest among the workers ..."

He put the letter down, looked up and with a tightly controlled face said to the Royal Valet, "You know the workers – what does this mean?"

The Royal Valet, who was from Household quickly composed himself and replied, "They say they're demotivated, they say they've got no idea what the Court does nor what it wants to do in the future. They say that there's not enough communication and no one listens to them. They'd also like more money."

"What!" exploded the Lord Chamberlain. "But they're doing the same job that they've done for centuries! And I talk to them all the time!"

"And that's another thing," the Royal Valet replied, "they want job rotations with the Knights."

※※※※※※※

As the Royal Valet left his office, the Lord Chamberlain noticed the small boy in front of him. The Lord Chamberlain looked at the boy and raised his eyebrows in question.

"I've come to learn sir," the boy said. "Can I watch?"

"What ... oh all right," he muttered and waved the boy towards a corner, "but stay out of the way."

The small boy sat and watched. And sat and watched.

People came and went, not noticing him as he sat so quietly. Finally, the great man rose from his desk and stretched, reflecting on the day's events and planning the next. Suddenly he remembered his charge and looked over to him, unmoving in the corner.

"Come and have something to eat and drink," he said, indicating the food and liquid on this desk, "and tell me what you have learnt."

"Thank you sir," the boy responded, "and I will. But to tell you the truth, I'm not sure of what I've learnt today. Could you answer a question?"

"Of course," replied the Lord Chamberlain smiling, "but first ..." indicating the meal.

The boy took a bite of bread and then took up his goblet of water. Bringing the liquid to his lips he said, "you are told many things Sir. How do you know what's important and needs dealing with, and what should be ignored?"

The Lord Chamberlain stopped for a second, smiled and said, "Well boy, it all comes down to having a vision and a strategy to achieve that vision. Anything that doesn't contribute to the strategy can be ignored. Let me tell you a story ..."

The Presentation

The man looked out across the sea of faces and smiled. By rights he had nothing to smile about – today was critical to the continued existence of his new organisation – but he couldn't help it. Twenty-five years of experience had led him to this moment.

"It's good to see so many here," his assistant John said stepping up to stand next to him, "and all the important ones at that."

"Yes," the man replied, "we have a good chance."

John stepped away and busied himself behind the lectern, making sure that everything was right for the man.

In time, the crowd settled. The man walked quietly towards the back of the stage, and waited for John to introduce him.

"Ladies and gentlemen," John began, his voice booming across the auditorium, "there is much I could say about the main speaker tonight, but I fear that mere words would not be enough. Therefore, can I simply introduce, the man who will take us forward!"

Polite applause rippled through the auditorium.

"An interesting start," the man thought. "Oh well, here we go..."

Stepping up to the lectern, he glanced down at his notes, and stopped. Looking up again at the audience, he paused, and moved to the front of the stage.

"Ladies and gentlemen." he began. "I came here tonight with a prepared speech. However, looking at you all, I now know it's not what's needed. Instead," he continued, "I want to talk to you from my heart. I want to share what I believe to be true and what I believe is our future. I may not be as slick, or say all the right words, but what you will hear is real to me."

The man stopped, fiddled briefly with his cufflinks, then continued.

"As you know, this organisation – *your* organisation – is in trouble. I have been asked by the Board to come, take a look, and make my recommendations. Well, I've been here three months now and before I take my proposals to the Board, I wanted to share them with you. You, every single one of you, are a key part of this organisation and without your support we have no chance of success."

"We are currently in trouble. We are losing money every day and if we don't do something, we will be bankrupt by the end of the year. I must emphasise this point – if we do nothing then we will be closed by the end of the year."

The audience murmured their disquiet.

The man raised his hands. "'Why are we in such a state?' you may ask. Well, answers are never clear but I'll try and give you the main reasons:

"One. We're spending money that we haven't got. There are many reasons for this; promises made by other organisations that haven't been kept, forecasts made that haven't been realised, projects needing more money than planned, to name but a few. However, the reality is, we're spending too much money.

"Two. Our income is not high enough. In the past, we simply believed that providing a service was enough. It's not anymore. We need to find new income streams and different customers.

"Three. Many of our existing customers don't think we do enough for them. Again, in the past this didn't matter. But customers now have a choice, and they're not choosing us.

"Four. Many of our people aren't committed to us. When we were the only player in town, we were always able to hire enough new blood to replace the leavers. However, the whole country is facing a shortage of skilled professionals and we now can't even hire the 'barely–adequates'.

"So where does this leave us?"

The man paused, slowly surveying the audience. A low hum of expectant voices filled his ears.

"Well, I must admit, it might be easier to tell the Board to 'close it',"

The man paused for effect.

"But I have a cunning plan."

He smiled.

"Now this plan involves pain, it involves hard work and it involves making tough decisions. But most of all it involves you. Without *your* help, this plan will not work."

The hubbub from the auditorium increased in tempo.

"Let me tell you what I think we should do," he continued.

"In the short term, we need to stop losing money. To this extent, I propose that all non-critical projects be stopped. This may mean leaving initiatives half implemented, but better that than having no business!

"I also propose that we have a hiring freeze wherever possible – three months only, not long, but long enough to get ourselves in good enough shape to sell the organisation honestly to the next person we hire. Finally, there's some short term funding that we can get from the government that will help.

"This is important stuff and it will ensure our survival, but the real plan starts with knowing who we are and what services we provide. Therefore, we, all of us, need to engage in agreeing what our future looks like, who our customers are, what they want and why they would come to us rather than the competition.

"Why, you may ask yourself, do we need to bother? 'Why, if he can make the books balance, do we need to do all this other stuff?'

"Well, the answer is simple. Because if we don't, we will be back here again next year, or the year after, in the same position."

The man stepped off the stage and onto the floor of the auditorium. The noise level instantly rose at this unexpected gesture of informality.

"Unless we can articulate why we exist and what we stand for – our vision and values – we will always be condemned to struggling to survive. If we take our vision and values and create a strategy – a plan of how we will achieve our vision in a way that holds true to our values – we will have a roadmap for the future. That roadmap will allow us to allocate our resources appropriately; remain unique and different from our competitors; measure our performance, as a team and as individuals, and prepare for the future. Most importantly, it will give all of us a sense of purpose and direction that has been lacking – a common message that we can share with each other, with customers and with other stakeholders.

"Because, ladies and gentleman, the key to making any plan successful is 'the four Cs' – communication, consistency, credibility and commitment.

"*Communication* means exactly that – you, me, *all of us* need to communicate the plan whenever we have the opportunity.

"*Consistency* sounds obvious but can be the hardest to achieve – making sure that we all, individually and collectively, tell the same message so that our listeners hear the same story.

"*Credibility* means that what we tell others has to make sense – the plan has to be realistic and achievable. It also means that when others hear the consistent message, they know we're all committed and believe in the message.

"Finally, *commitment* means that we need to act on the plan and do our bit, however large or small, to ensure it's successful."

The man hesitated, catching his breath. His audience paused in anticipation of his next words.

"I said earlier that it might be easier if I simply told the Board to close the doors and shut the organisation down but do you know why I won't?"

Silence met the man's question.

"I won't, simply because of you. If you are prepared to brave this meeting hall in such numbers and show such concern for this supposedly 'terminally dead' organisation," the man briefly paused, "then we are capable of doing anything!"

The clapping began, slowly at first but increasing with every heartbeat. Gathering momentum, the audience rose to its feet, cheering and stamping as the man raised his arms in triumph.

"Parents, guardians and governors," he shouted, "this will become the best school in the country."

The boy looked thoughtful.

The Lord Chamberlain waited.

"So," the boy started, "what the man is saying, is that when an organisation knows where it wants to get to, it can build a plan to help it get there. And a plan lets you know what's important and what's not."

"That's right," the Lord Chamberlain nodded, "a vision and set of values allows an organisation to create a plan or strategy, and having a strategy means that people can concentrate on the important things that make a difference."

He continued, "A strategy can also bring people together to work as a team and allow them to talk consistently amongst themselves and to a wider audience. Which in turn helps give the strategy credibility and drives personal commitment."

The boy turned and walked towards the door, "Hmm. Thank you, I still have much to learn ..."

The Keeper of the Privy Purse's View

The Keeper of the Privy Purse heard the commotion from the Lord Chamberlain's office and let a wry smile cross her lips. "Must have just heard about the field workers," she mused. Her smile faded. She'd told him months ago that something was wrong – the numbers never lied – but he'd been hard pressed to find the time to investigate it.

She turned to more pressing matters, that of ensuring that the gods had the right offerings for the next quarter. The news was not good; production levels were down and although she could balance existing stock levels for at least two more quarters, she knew that the future wasn't bright.

Worse still, since her assistant had left, she'd had to make do with two less experienced replacements. "If I'd had my way, I'd have increased the retirement age," she muttered, "that would have kept him here." The Keeper of the Privy Purse also thanked the gods that she'd both insisted that her assistant document everything in the months before he left and that they'd invested in the latest information system to ensure the handover was as smooth as possible.

At least the rest of her team were in good spirits. Not that the Keeper of the Privy Purse rested on her laurels – she always had her spies out looking for potential assistants in the enemy camps. It was a risky business that took time, cunning, a lot of gold and could also bring dishonour if done badly but high rewards if done well.

A breeze moved across her desk, disturbing her papers. Looking around for the source, she noticed the young boy. "How did you get in here?" she asked. "And why?"

The boy looked at the Keeper of the Privy Purse and smiled.

"Oh you must be the Page they were going to send," she said, answering her own question.

"Well I've nothing for you at the moment so sit over there and watch."

"Certainly ma'am," he replied, "but ..."

"But, what?" the Keeper of the Privy Purse *snapped.*

"Could you tell me how you are able to get so much done?" he said.

"What?" the Keeper of the Privy Purse looked again at the young boy. "What do you mean ... oh, why am I so productive?"

The boy nodded at the Keeper of the Privy Purse and smiled.

The Keeper of the Privy Purse stopped for a second, smiled and said, "Well boy, it all comes down to having the right people and giving them clear focus and the right tools. Let me tell you a story ..."

The Legacy

THE OPPORTUNITY

Once upon a time, a woman inherited a business from a distant relative. It was a good business; it made a small profit, employed a few people, was supported by a number of suppliers and had a good reputation in its marketplace.

"In fact," the woman thought, "I could do something with this." So she hired a friend to look at the business and come to her with recommendations for its future.

The friend asked for a month to look at the company. At the end of the period he came back to her with a glowing report.

"The potential is great," he said, "but you'll need to consider a new distribution channel. Your current model is restricted by the number of people you have and they can never hope to meet the demand that I could create with more proactive marketing. I recommend that you invest heavily early on to gain the greatest benefits."

The woman thought about this for a while.

"What do our customers say about this approach?" she said.

"I've not asked them," her friend replied, "because they'll soon be in the minority."

"What about the staff?"

"I've not asked them either," her friend replied, "because they don't have the skills to implement the new model. They will only feel threatened and disagree with everything I say."

"And what of your marketing projections – are they sound?"

"They are based on extensive research," her friend replied, "from both this and other countries. I have surveyed your competitors and similar industries, and I feel confident that I can achieve the targets I've put in my recommendations."

"When will the investment pay for itself?"

"Within the year." her friend replied. "Eighteen months at the worst."

The woman thought some more.

"Okay," she said. "You can have the money, and my support to implement your recommendations."

THE CRISIS – PART ONE

Twelve months later, the woman found her friend back in front of her.

"How's the business?" she asked, expecting good news.

"It's going well," he replied, "but I need to invest more money to maximise the expected benefits."

"Expected benefits? Are you not making a profit?"

"No," he replied, "but I still have six more months remember. Anyway, business is harder than expected and customers are not using the new distribution channel as much as we need them to. However, the good news is that we've attracted a new type of customer – one who's prepared to pay more for our products."

"What do they want in return?"

"Better service," he replied, "which is why we need to spend more money ensuring the distribution channel is running 24/7. Anyway, we were too reliant in the past on the repeat business of a few small customers – now we have the opportunity to offer a wider product range."

"What about the staff?"

"Great news," he replied. "I've tripled the headcount and we're still working all hours to get the products out." The man laughed, "you could say I was 'sweating the resources'."

"But you've still not repaid the investment?"

"No," he replied, "but we still have six months."

The woman thought about this for a while.

"Okay," she said, "you can have the money, and my support to implement your recommendations."

THE CRISIS – PART TWO

Six months later, the woman asked her manager to see her.

"How's the business?" she asked.

"It's going well," he replied, "but I need to invest more money to take advantage of a new opportunity."

"Are you making a profit?"

"No," the manager replied, "but the environment has changed remember. Business is harder than expected and customers don't have the cash to buy our products, even though our distribution channel is the best in the market. However, the good news is that we've attracted a new type of customer – one who doesn't want to pay as much for our products but is far more loyal."

"So why do you need more money?"

"To spend on customer services staff," the manager replied, "to make sure the new customers remain loyal."

The woman thought about this for a while.

"No," she said, "you can't have the money and you don't have my support to implement your recommendations. And I'll tell you why..."

THE REPOSITIONING

"Have you spoken to the staff recently?" the woman asked.

"No," replied the manager, shaking his head. "What chance do I have? Anyway, it's more important that we look after the customers."

"Those same customers that we had eighteen months ago?"

"What do you mean?" the manager replied.

"I've spoken to the staff recently," the woman went on, "and do you know what they said?"

The manager shook his head.

"It turns out they weren't against implementing the new distribution channel, in fact they thought it was a good idea. It also turns out that they had been pestering my dear departed relative to do much the same thing before I came to own the business.

"But what they also said was that although you've wasted a lot of money on things that the market wasn't ready for, we are better positioned than our competitors for future growth. Furthermore, with only a few small investments in software technology, they believe that they could double their current productivity overnight.

"Like you, they also believe there is a huge opportunity to go after customers who are prepared to pay more for a better service, but, as you have recently been discovering, they believe that we should not forget our traditional customer base – those people who are more price conscious but will keep coming back time after time.

"What they want however is job clarity. Those people who are good with our traditional customers don't always have the skills to deal with the new ones and vice versa – they want to stop covering both types and focus on one.

"They also want to know what's expected of them – they think they could do a better job if you tell them what's important – is it an efficient distribution channel or customers? They don't mind, they know both are important but just tell them what this business values more.

"Finally, they want to be able to talk to you and for you to listen. They would have told you all of this eighteen months ago, but you didn't give them a chance. They would have told you that your ideas were good, but that they'd already experienced the fickle nature of the new customer base and that we need to keep a regular revenue stream coming in.

"If you talk to them now, they'll tell about what our biggest competitor is doing, and boy is that a concern, but they'll also tell you about a potential new product they believe will knock the spots of them."

The woman stopped talking and looked at her manager.

He opened his mouth and then shut it. Gulping he asked, "Am I sacked?"

THE OPPORTUNITY REVISITED

"No."

The man looked at the woman.

"No." Shaking her head, the woman said, "Why would I sack you, having spent all this money on training you? However, things have to change.

"First, no more money except what little is needed to buy the software to increase staff productivity.

"Second, you need to restructure the team to focus them on your two defined customer bases.

"Third, you need to focus on what this company stands for – is it customers, efficiency or innovation? All three are important but one has to be the primary driver."

"Lastly, you have to listen. We could have got to this point twelve months ago had you listened to the staff and incorporated their comments into your strategy."

The manager looked at his friend and smiled. "I think I can do that," he said, "let's get to work."

※※※※※※※

The Keeper of the Privy Purse finished her story and looked at the boy.

"What do think the man learnt from the woman?" she asked.

"Well," he replied, "people are very important, but they need to know what they're doing. Also," he continued, "they work much better if you make their job easier for them to do. Like the software and the new channel she talked about."

"Good," said the Keeper of the Privy Purse, "but don't forget, people normally know their job better than you ever will. Once they know where they're going, they'll often know the best way to get there."

"Thank you," the boy said, " there is still so much I need to learn …"

The Master of The Household's View

The Master of the Household lifted his weary head. He had sent the Royal Valet into the Lord Chamberlain's office with a sense of foreboding – he fared he would be held responsible for not anticipating the workers' unrest. It was hardly his fault; he didn't even know what they did!

He glanced down at his 'to do' list. The usual things, recruitment here, a bit of development there, advice to managers about 'the law' and ensuring they followed 'the rules' (which he had spent days putting together!) He had a good team – his organisation was 'modern' with a shared service centre and business partners, and he'd started to call them specialists. "That should keep them motivated," he thought.

But somewhere, in the back of his head, a tiny thought kept nagging him. "What if I've got this wrong," it said, casting doubt within a man at the top of his profession. "What if there is another way?"

The Master of the Household got up from his desk and went to look out of his window. He smiled as he surveyed the view.

"The rewards of high office," he said to himself, only half in jest. Lost in thought, he made his way back to his desk, not seeing the young boy until he had almost stepped on him.

"Oh, sorry!" he said looking down. "How did you get there?"

"Excuse me sir," the boy responded, "but could you answer a question for me?"

"I'll try," the Master of the Household replied. "What is it?"

"Why are people so important?"

The Master of the Household stopped for a second, smiled and said, "Well boy, people are important, but it's just as critical to have the right talent and be able to motivate it. Let me tell you a story ..."

The One Sided Conversation

Hi there. Come on in, did you want to chat?

No problems, happy to help. Pull up a seat – I'll just finish this work and come around to the table.

There – thanks for waiting. How's life – still knocking them dead at Corporate?

That's great. Yeah, I'm okay – same old stuff. As you know, we're in the planning stage for the upcoming reviews and despite what you and your peers say, my team do need to put a lot of work into it to give you something resembling 'fact' in a month's time. Once that's over, we'll be into the process proper and then comes budgets...

I know, I know, it never stops.

Anyway, what can I do for you?

You want to talk about a personal matter? Okay, what's on your mind?

Thinking about your career with the company? What do you mean exactly?

Let me get this straight. You're wondering about your next job, whether the company loves you and what the future holds?

So that's a good summary?

Okay. So let's go through the basics. Firstly, you're on the 'fast-track' programme, one of only 100 from this Division. That's 1% you know. Secondly, you were asked to head up a company wide project team, reporting into the CEO – of the company, not our Division – and report back to her on what we need to do better to cross sell the company's products. Thirdly, this project has attracted the attention of the Chairman – it's a hot issue with Investors – and you're hitting all your project deliverables. Fourthly, am I up to four? The recent employee survey shows that your staff love you. Finally, at least until I can think of another reason for you to be happy, is that you're exceeding your targets, under budget and should have a great year.

So which bit of this shows the company either doesn't love you or doesn't think you can do your job?

So what is the issue?

Yes, I'm aware of that conversation.

Are you concerned that my boss is being underhanded, or that the individual he was referring to shouldn't be moved out of this current job, or that you couldn't do that role if you were to be offered it?

All of the above? Hmm, so do you think the current individual is doing the job well?

No, okay, so you think someone else should do the job, but not you?

No. I agree, I think you could bring a new passion to the role, and we've discussed your ideas often enough for me to be totally confident you can deliver. Who do you think pushed the MD so hard? Yeah, it's a big role, an order of magnitude bigger than your current one, but the size of your team is the same and your passion and ability to communicate with all levels of the organisation is the critical skill that's needed.

No false modesty please. This is important and we need to get to the bottom of it. I'll tell you what your faults are soon enough; you need to be frank with me.

Okay, thank you. Now, where were we? Oh yes – so you think that change is needed, you have clear ideas about what needs to happen and the company thinks you've got the skills to do it.

You agree. So what you're really worried about is the fact that our boss, well your boss to be, has been underhand?

In what way?

What do I mean – in what way? Well, do you think he should have taken the current incumbent through the disciplinary process, or, do you think the role should be advertised, or, what? Because, well you know that if the role becomes available, it will be advertised. Just because you've been told about it in advance ... well, we both know you haven't really ...

So you're not sure why you're unhappy? Do you like your current role?

Oh.

Ah. I think I see part of your problem. You haven't delivered what you wanted to deliver and now you're moving on. Well, you've got an important job currently but, at the end of the day, you're only supporting the revenue generating parts of the business. I know you find that quite novel but in the new role, well you will be the main man – or should I say 'main person' in case HR is listening.

Hmmm.

How are the kids by the way?

Yeah, they are aren't they? Do you get the chance to see them regularly?

That's tough.

Hmmm.

Can I ask you a question?

Where do you want to be in five and in ten years time?

Not doing this eh?

What would you want to be doing?

That sounds wonderful. Could you afford it?

Yeah, true. Once those two costs are out of the way and you're no longer responsible for the little ones, you're probably right.

You've really thought this through haven't you?

Does the boss know any of this?

At last, we come to the issue at hand.

What do you mean 'what do I mean?' You know exactly what I'm talking about. This whole conversation isn't about the new role or whether you could do it – you know you can. This conversation is about whether you *want* to do it, about the impact on your current life outside of work and whether it will get you to your future dream life.

No, no, I understand. It's not that you hate your current role or the new role or the company. It's about personal control and ownership, it's about being asked and not told, about being your own person and not becoming the corporate animal you so hate.

Well my friend, that is an altogether different conversation.

As the Master of the Household finished his story the boy hopped down from where he was sitting.

"That person was talking to someone good wasn't he?"

The Master of the Household nodded.

"And yet this person was unhappy," he continued, "is it because he was being told what to do and not being asked?"

"Yes," The Master of the Household nodded. "Individual people are critical to organisations being successful and the right person in the right role can make an enormous difference. However," he continued, "people are not robots and will not just do as they're told willingly. You need to motivate them, understand their individual needs, help them feel part of the organisation and work with them to find the best way of achieving their part in reaching the organisation's vision."

The boy looked up at the Master of the Household. "Thank you. I am learning so much ..."

The Steward's View

The Steward snarled at the delegation sent from the fields. "What do you want now?"

The three men and single woman stopped at the edge of the Steward's desk. They smiled hesitantly before looking to the most senior in their party. She stepped forward.

"Come on then, spit it out," the Steward said, "I haven't got all day!"

"We've come to see whether you're going to respond to our demands," she said.

"Like hell I am!" he muttered under his breath. Speaking up he said, "I've sent them to the Lord Chamberlain – is that good enough?"

"Thank you," she answered, "we'll await his response."

As the delegation trooped out of his office, the Steward sat back in his chair and sighed. "I didn't want this job," he thought, "but how else am I going to get a decent pay rise? If they'd only leave me alone for long enough to let me get to the senior Steward's role," his thoughts continued, "I'd never have to deal with these people again."

Glancing around he saw the young boy.

"Who ..." he began and stopped. "Are you one of them?" he went on.

The boy shook his head.

"Then what are you doing?" the Steward asked.

"The Queen said I could watch and learn," the young boy said, "and I'd like to ask you a question."

The Steward thought for a moment. "Well," he began, "if the Queen said it's okay, then it must be alright." He paused, gathering strength, "What's your question?"

"What do you do?"

The Steward stopped for a second, smiled and said, "Well boy, it all comes down to managing resources and competing demands in order to *achieve everyone's goals. It's also about recognising that things change and the right action yesterday may not be the right response tomorrow. Let me tell you a story ..."*

The Man

BUILDING THE VISION

A man had a dream to become the best in his profession.

However, his ambitions ran ahead of his experience and the organisations that he joined or sought to join were quick to dispense of him or turn him away. The reasons were varied – not the right 'fit', too aggressive, not enough experience, too much experience – but the underlying message was clear:

> **"Know your place,
> don't buck the system."**

In time, the man gathered enough knowledge to set up his own business, begging and borrowing finances to begin to make his dream a reality. It was tough at first; the establishment didn't like new competition and the man had to fight to stay in the game.

However, over time, he attracted the support that comes to the underdog, collecting like-minded people around him who helped him to grow his customer base.

The press came to notice that he was fighting and winning the battle against the entrenched interests. The man became admired as a believer in innovation and risk taking.

Having attracted the attention of the wider community, the man issued a challenge to the establishment – "I will become number one!"

MAKING THE VISION REALITY

The establishment joined forces to fight the newcomer.

Some took him on directly and sought to undercut his prices. But the man used his new-found power with the press to appeal directly to their shareholders and the authorities.

Others sought to bring him into their fold, offering riches beyond his wildest dreams. But the man had learnt from his earlier experiences not to trust such offers.

A few tried to improve their product range, seeking to match what the man already offered his customers. But the man kept improving his products and the competitors weren't as quick or nimble and couldn't keep up.

The man weathered the storm and in time counter attacked. Quietly, he started to acquire his smaller competitors. Although initially many times his size, his reputation now worked in his favour and both investors and employees were quick to support his ventures.

The trickle became a flood as one after another of the competitors were acquired, first locally, then nationally and finally internationally.

Eventually, the man stopped to survey his empire. He could remember the hard days, the difficult days, the days when whichever direction he turned, he faced potential ruin.

Now he looked out on the biggest business in his marketplace – an international business that ranked amongst the world's greats and a story of how it was made that would be retold for years to come.

And for a while, the man was happy.

THE VISION STAGNATES…

Investors and commentators, having watched on as the man's business became an international giant, started to raise their concerns.

"What will you do next?"

"Will you consolidate your acquisitions?"

"What about cost efficiencies?"

Employees too started to voice their concerns.

"How do I earn my next bonus?"

"What can I do now?"

"Who is going to manage the business?"

The sole remaining Competitor, the only other business in the marketplace that had kept up with the man, started to use *his* media tactics.

"This is not good for the customer."

"What about all the job losses?"

"This is too much power in one person's hands."

The man ignored these voices initially, but as the noise level grew, turned to face his tormentors.

"I am number one! I am the best there is! Why can't you see that and leave me alone!"

...AND TOPPLES

But they didn't.

His closest managers, so supportive of each other during the tough times and then during the expansion, turned their skills inwards, seeking to increase their own personal empires.

The new acquisitions, lacking direction and clarity, sought refuge in their previous plans, often at the expense of their now sister divisions.

Employees, having no affinity with the 'new' organisation but realising that their old organisation had gone, aligned themselves as best they could – to their workgroup, their division and to their 'star managers'.

Slowly, the organisation turned into a series of fiefdoms, where loyalty was given to and rewarded by individuals. Lacking clear boundaries, these fiefdoms were often at war with each other and the single remaining competitor became less important to those inside the organisation.

Customers were ignored – although they were often a rallying call for the latest battle.

The organisation dropped to number two.

In time, the man realised that building the business was only part of the dream – he also had to make sure that his business stayed at the top. For the first time in his life he turned his attention inwards, seeking to capture the spirit of the early days.

Bringing together the senior team that he'd kept with him from the beginning, he started to issue commands:

"You run this and do that!"

"You achieve this by the end of the next quarter!"

But employees no longer believed in the vision. They'd been there, they realised it wasn't nirvana and they'd moved on to other priorities.

Some managers realised that the organisation needed a new vision. When presented with the evidence the man acted quickly, firing the ringleaders and demoting others. Dissent became risky.

Lacking a unifying vision, money became the new enabler. Employees who were critical to the organisation gained both financial rewards and public recognition − promotions, bigger cars and grander titles. At the top of the organisation, it became financially difficult to leave the organisation and even more difficult to change 'the winning formula'.

Investors, once friends, judged the business harshly. The vision had become a millstone around the neck of the organisation.

THE NEW DAY COMES?

In a part of the organisation far from the core, the first rays of enlightenment began to dawn. They had seen how the organisation had become great and how it had stumbled. They saw the fiefdoms, the lack of controls, the overdependence on a few individuals and the costs required to maintain the creaking system. They also knew the culture and the history. Importantly, they knew the man; his drives, his vision and his weaknesses, and they had already built his trust.

Slowly, they gathered people around them with a different mindset, with talents that were rare in the organisation but judged critical to future success. This process was difficult – the organisation put up constant blockers to stop these people using their talents to the best of their ability – but the new recruits were constantly reminded of the new world and most persisted. The new order were savvy, they didn't threaten the organisation's core with their new mode of working, even if that meant taking a longer route to achieve their goals.

Eventually, the first tipping point was passed and the investment started to bring visible rewards. The new order turned up the heat, the trickle of new talent became a flood, supporting the existing vision but with a different way of operating.

The man, at last alerted to the existence of the new order, looked out upon that part of his organisation. Concerned, he called the senior members to him and asked them to justify themselves. Listening to their answers and judging their results, he was content with what they'd done but insisted they go no further.

The new order listened, and planned their next move.

※※※

The boy smiled as the Steward finished his story. "This is a story about a man who came from nothing to be the best," he said. "But I don't understand what happened."

The Steward returned the smile. "What happened was that although the man had a personal vision to be number one, when that vision was achieved, he couldn't provide a subsequent one for the organisation."

"So he went from being the hero to the villain then?" the boy asked.

"Yes, you could put it like that," the Steward responded. "From a situation of using everything in his power to become number one, he didn't recognise that those skills and that knowledge would not sustain him once he was there. He needed to manage his resources

in a different way, but couldn't or wouldn't make the change.

The boy turned to leave, stopped and looked back. "Thank you. I think it's becoming clearer now ..."

The Royal Valet's View

"Fools," he exclaimed as he walked away from the Lord Chamberlain's office, "both of them! They don't care about anything other than the next quarter's offerings! If I was in charge, I'd look after the things that really matter..."

He stopped as he noticed the young boy directly in front of him. "Hello," he said, "are you okay?"

"My name is Janus," the boy said, "and I'd like to be a King. Can you teach me?"

"That's a lot to ask," laughed the Royal Valet, "why do you want to know how to be a King?"

"My mother works in the fields," Janus replied, "and she's unhappy. I want to help and I thought that if I became King, I could make her problems go away."

The Royal Valet looked thoughtfully at the boy. "Why do you think I'll be able to help you?" he asked.

"You see and hear so much," Janus said. "You must surely have a view on what goes on."

The Royal Valet smiled, thought for a moment and then guided the young boy to an unoccupied office.

"Well, it all comes down to giving direction and enabling people to do the best job that they can. Let me tell you a story ..."

The Meeting

THE ISSUE

An unhappy man found time in his busy schedule to stop and reflect on the last thirty days of his life. He knew he should be happy but somehow the smile didn't come to his face.

Acting on impulse he grabbed his coat and phone and headed outside being careful to avoid his assistants on the way. "I'm just taking a break," he said as they looked up from their desk, "I'll be back before my next meeting."

Pausing for breath as he reached the pavement, he looked left and then right, deciding which way to go. Remembering the little park nearby, he crossed the road and made his way towards it.

On entering the park, he saw a bench and headed for it. Only when he sat down did he notice the old woman sitting next to him. "Sorry," he said, and got up to leave.

"Stay if you wish," she replied, putting a hand on his leg, "I'd like the company and besides," she added, "if you've got the time then you could help me enjoy this beautiful day."

"Sorry?" he said.

"Beauty, like a problem, is always better shared," she explained. "Look! See the robin darting in among the trees over there."

Following her pointing arm, he watched the little bird flittering back and forth. They sat for a short while; silently watching various small animals come and go. The morning sun shone brightly and the man eased himself into the bench, letting the tension leave him.

In time, he looked at his watch, sighed, and got up to go.

"You seem disturbed young man," the woman said. "We have shared beauty this morning – do you want to share your troubles too?"

"Thank you for your kind offer," the man said, "and I have enjoyed your company but my troubles ... well, I find it hard to explain them to myself, let alone to others. I will be fine."

"I've no doubt that you will," she replied, "and I'm sure I can offer you no advice but I promise that I won't judge you and the sun can only do you good. Stay a while and humour an old lady."

The man looked at his watch, thought for a moment, reached into his coat pocket to turn off his mobile phone and sat back down on the bench.

"It sounds silly," he began, "but I should be the happiest man on earth. I was recently promoted to the job I've always wanted and yet I'm now beginning to think I can't do it."

"It seems like it started so long ago," he continued, "when I was responsible for creating my company's strategy. It was, and still is, a good strategy. Based on excellent research, well thought through scenarios and achievable goals. My colleagues and I agreed it was the right thing for the company." The man shrugged, "the Board said yes and I thought, 'we're off'."

"For a little while things went okay, no, *well*. But it became obvious over time that despite the support of senior management, we just weren't doing it."

"Doing what?" asked the old woman.

"Achieving our goals," the man said. "I mean the strategy was good, the plans were clear and we communicated really well, but ...

"Anyway, I was passionate about it so I went on the warpath, started to cajole and harangue the Board and my colleagues, but to no avail. At that point I started to play the 'game', inferring it was my boss's fault, that I could do better, all I needed was the chance."

"But ...?" continued his companion.

"Well, I got my chance a month ago." He shrugged again. "Yet here I sit, unable to do any better than old Harry, the CEO I've replaced."

"Do you know why he was failing?" the woman asked.

"Yes," the man smiled. "One of the benefits of the new job was that I could find that out. I immediately commissioned a lot of research and they found, essentially, that people weren't doing what we asked them to do."

"Why not?"

"I don't know."

"Why not?" the women gently asked.

The man sat for a while.

"Have you asked them?" the woman continued. "Have you put yourself in their shoes?"

"No."

"What might they say?"

"I don't know."

DELIVERING THE ROLE

"Why did you want your job?" the woman asked.

"Well," the man paused, "I thought I could do it."

"Why were you given the job?"

"They thought I had the ability, skills and the vision to implement the strategy."

"Were you born with those skills and abilities?"

"No." The man laughed. "I understand what you're saying – I've learnt them over my career – my life. You're right, of course, I shouldn't expect myself to have all of the answers right now, but ..." The man shrugged his shoulders.

"What about your assistants?" she asked.

"What about them?" he replied.

"Could they do your job?"

"No!" His face paled. "What do you mean?"

"Could you do theirs?"

"Sorry?" He looked quizzically at the woman.

"Would you tell them how to do their job?" the woman continued.

"Well, no. I'd tell them what I expected as an output, but I'd expect them to know how to achieve it," the man thought for a second, "unless they couldn't for some reason and then I'd expect them to talk to me about it. If it was a reasonable excuse, I'd see it as my job to help them fix the problem."

"What if they were new to their role?"

"Well, I'd expect them to develop over time. If they needed support or training or such like, well, they'd get it."

"And eventually they could do your job?"

"No, of course not. They'd develop *their* skills, experience and abilities in ways specific to *their* job. But their, well talents I suppose, would be focused on their role and roles like theirs. Eventually they'd get to a point where they'd have little left to learn."

"And they would leave?"

"Some would. Others would look to stay, or become a mentor to others, or change jobs."

"Why would some stay and others not?"

"It depends on what's important to them – what their drivers are. If they have families, or want to be promoted, or security. Whatever."

"Or even if they wanted to do their dream job?"

"What? I don't understand." The man turned to look at the woman. "Oh, of course, like me. Yes, their dream job. So I suppose that makes them like me, but only different."

LEARNING TO ACCEPT HELP

"What are you thinking?" said the woman.

"Well," the man said, "I'm thinking that I shouldn't be too hard on myself and that I can't expect to have all the answers. But this hasn't solved my problem yet, just made me feel better!"

"So in time you'll have all the answers then?"

"No, of course not. But in time, I'll be better at making decisions based on the information I get."

"And how do you get that information?"

"Systems, technology, well people I suppose."

"But those systems can't tell you why your employees aren't doing what you ask of them?"

"No."

"And what if you didn't have your technology, what then?"

"Well, technology makes communication easier."

"Ah, so it's communication then."

"Yeah, I reckon so."

"And technology, what else does it do?"

"Well it makes jobs easier. It's like having standard processes ..."

"And structure?"

"Structure? Organisational structure?" The man paused, thinking for a moment. "Yes, you're right, the right organisational structure should make achieving objectives easier."

"So, if your assistants had typewriters, had to change the format of each letter they typed and reported into the office junior, you'd expect them to do less work?"

"Yes," he said laughing, "I would."

"And if they worked in a company that didn't tolerate mistakes, punished people for speaking up, or rewarded longevity and not productivity?"

"Well ..."

"And personal power, the size of your desk and the number of employees that reported to you was more important than company survival?"

"Yes."

A breeze swept across the park, making the man shudder.

"Now what are you thinking?" asked the woman.

"That employees not only need the right tools, right processes and the right structure in order to their job, but the company culture and its values also need to be right."

THE NEED FOR CONSISTENT REINFORCEMENT

"You mentioned communication," said the woman.

"Did I? Oh yes, I did. In what context?"

"In the context of getting the information you need to do your job. Or, as you put it, to make decisions."

"Oh yes." The man thought for a while. "I suppose in the context of what we're talking about, we all need information to do our jobs."

The woman remained silent.

"But ... in fact, thinking about it, I need communication to be a two-way process – sharing my vision and getting feedback about what works and what doesn't work. The issue is therefore about ensuring I get the right information from the right sources and making sure they see and hear my vision." The man closed his eyes, looked upwards and smiled. "Hallelujah!"

He sprang to his feet and turned to thank the woman. As he opened his mouth, the woman raised an eyebrow and asked, "Why didn't Harry think of that?"

The man stopped, mouth agape. And sat down again.

"I ..." he stammered, "don't know."

"A question for you," the woman replied. "Who is more important in an individual's daily life; their manager or the latest memo from 'headquarters'; the process they've always followed or the new manual on their desk; the latest gossip or the latest press release; their current performance objectives or the latest strategy paper?

"You think that communication involves only written words?" she finished.

The Importance of Communication

"So," the man said, "what you're saying is that every communication that touches an employee has to be the same message?"

"No," she said, "what I'm saying is that there are more powerful influences than the written word. You simply need to use them, work with them and certainly make sure they don't work against you. Anyway, that's assuming that everyone believes you."

"But why wouldn't they? Our strategy is logical and well thought through. In fact our biggest competitor looks likely to try the same thing."

"I thought you said earlier that employees are human too?" replied the woman.

"Oh, of course," he said. "You're right. Different perspectives drive different views.

"Oh god," the man continued, "we need to do this. Our competitors are knocking at our door, our customers are already beginning to doubt our commitment and our staff don't trust me."

"But is your strategy sound?"

"What ... well yes, I truly believe so."

"So ...?"

"So I need to ensure that my employees come to the same conclusion as me. And once they do, make sure that they keep getting the same message from other information sources as well."

BRINGING IT ALL TOGETHER

"What if your employees didn't have the skills, knowledge or experience or the talent as you call it, to do their job?" the woman asked.

"Well, I'd either train them, or move them ... or sack them and hire someone who could," the man responded.

"So what talents are required to implement your strategy then?"

"Well it depends on ..." the man stopped. "You know, I don't know," he finished. "Isn't that ..."

"So you have a strategy," the woman filled the silence, "but you don't know what talent your company needs to implement it?"

"Or even what we've got at the moment," the man admitted.

"So how can you train, move, hire or fire someone without understanding whether they've got the talent to help you achieve your strategy? And once you know they've got the right talent, how do you make sure they've got the right tools, systems and structures in place to make their job easier? And once you have all of that, how do you ensure that your employees are committed to your vision and to the company?"

"Good questions," the man responded, "good questions."

The man looked at his watch again. Full of thought he got up and reached inside his coat pocket to turn his mobile on. Within seconds, the ringer went off. Glancing down, he noticed the caller and pressing the reply button, spoke briefly into the receiver. He started walking back to his office, but suddenly stopped, remembering where he was.

"I just wanted to say," he said, turning back to the old woman, and stopped. "Thanks." The words died away as he realised that there was no one on the bench. "Where did she …"

The mobile rang again. He looked at it, turned and hurried to his next meeting.

※※※※※※※※

The Royal Valet finished his story. "So you see," he continued, "being King is not about knowing all the answers. Being King is about making sure you know your direction, that your subjects know your direction and that they know their part in achieving it. It's then up to you to do everything in your power to ensure your subjects are supported in their personal quest to achieve those goals."

"I've been watching you on your travels in the Palace," the Royal Valet continued. *"Why don't you walk with me back to the Queen and tell her all you've discovered so far ..."*

The Boy's View

The Royal Valet and the boy started walking to the Queen's chambers.

"So you've learnt from my story," the Royal Valet began, "that while having a strategy is important, being able to implement it is even more so. And that ..." He stopped, noticing that the boy had raised his eyebrows. "Yes?"

"Where does 'vision' fit?" the boy asked.

The Royal Valet smiled. "Having a vision," he replied, "allows you to build a cohesive strategy. Think of it like a journey with a map – the vision is your destination while your strategy is the route you take to get there. You can have a strategy without a vision, but like a journey without a destination, you're likely to meander and never really know when you've arrived."

"Okay," the boy answered, nodding.

The Royal Valet waited and happy that the boy had understood, carried on. "However, people are the means by which a strategy is achieved. Unless they believe in the vision and agree with the strategy, they're unlikely to want to do anything differently from what they're already doing."

"And communicating the vision and strategy means having simple, consistent and continuous messages using all of the means that people ... well ... use to communicate with each other," the boy continued.

"That's right," the Royal Valet said, "but don't forget, people sometimes need help in understanding their role in supporting the vision and strategy."

"And don't forget the point about people needing the right skills and tools to do their jobs," batted back the boy, beaming as he started to get to grips with the information he was absorbing.

"Which you can extend to the processes, organisational structure, 'culture' and so on," the Royal Valet added.

"Culture?" the boy queried.

"Culture is a way of saying 'the way things are done in an organisation' – like common values, beliefs and behaviours. It's very hard to define and to demonstrate without pointing to specifics, but it's those things that help people believe they're part of the same organisation."

"Okay," the boy said warily. "Oh," he suddenly smiled again, "like the Christmas Party and the Queen giving presents to her staff each year?"

"Yes, and like the Queen never firing anyone and decisions taking forever to be made," the Royal Valet replied.

The boy looked thoughtful as he pondered the Royal Valet's words.

In silence, they continued walking towards the Queen's chambers.

The Queen, answering the knock at her door, summoned the boy in.

"Hello Janus, it's nice to see you again. Come in and tell me what you've learnt," she said, pointing to a chair by her side.

The boy settled himself in.

"I have learnt," he began, "that we do not have plenty of time because there are always dangers looming from both inside and outside the Palace gates.

"But I have also learnt," he added, "that while there are no right or wrong ways to deal with those dangers, the best responses are within our grasp. The kingdom has the ability to meet every danger, sometimes winning, often achieving honourable draws, and sometimes changing direction to avoid permanent damage. But always learning and developing on the journey to achieve our vision.

"The answer to every danger," he continued, "is simple. It's not about the best products, best customer relationships, best marketing plan or best processes; while important, these things are transient and not in our control for long.

"The answer to every danger comes from us. You, me, and our people. You simply have to give us a vision and the skills, tools and information to help you achieve it. And then trust us."

As the young boy walked away, the Queen glanced to her windows and noticed a storm building in the east – "Another challenge," she sighed. As she looked down at her work, she quietly murmured, "And when will any of us have the time to learn from the young?"

The Queen's Speech

Memorandum

To: Heads of Departments

From: Her Royal Majesty

Re: Draft Heads of Department Speech (excerpt only, includes speech and slides).

Action required: Comments to HRM as appropriate.

*...and I need to thank a young man whose quest for enlightenment has led me to realise some simple but powerful truths – truths that are at the heart of today's central message, a message that I call, **'achieving the vision'**.*

What I've come to realise is that an organisation's long-term ability to achieve its vision is solely dependent upon how it manages its talent and talent related activities.

Let me put it another way.

"Achieving the Vision"

An organisation's **vision** needs to be shared by its **employees** who have both the **talent** to do their jobs and who are allowed to be **effective** in achieving their own part of that vision.

In order to facilitate employee **effectiveness**, organisations need to **engage** with their employees, ensuring that they have the **capability** and **capacity** to do their jobs, and that they are supported by the organisation's **infrastructure**.

Organisations however need to recognise that individuals also have their own **personal drives** and desires. Influencing these needs can only come from understanding, acknowledging and then, where appropriate, meeting them.

Notice the words in bold.

Let me take those key words one by one and ask you some questions.

Vision

- *DO you know what our organisation's vision is?*
- *DO you know what your department's role is in achieving that vision?*

Employees

- *HAVE you got the right number of people to achieve our vision?*
- *HOW do you know?*

Talent

- DO you know what talent lies in your organisation?
- ARE you using that talent to its fullest potential?
- IS the talent you have what you need to achieve your part of the vision?

- IF you don't have the right talent, what are you doing to find it?

Effectiveness

- ARE our employees engaged with the organisation's vision?
- HOW do you know this?
- DO you know the true capability of your employees?
- CAN they do more than is currently being asked of them?
- DO you know what the most effective level of long–term, sustainable productivity is for your employees?
- DO your employees have the right systems and tools to do their jobs?
- DO your processes and organisational structures help or hinder employees in achieving their goals?

- DOES our culture and what we value support your employees in achieving our vision?

  Personal Drives

- DO you know what's important to your employees?

- HOW do you know?

- WHAT are you doing to positively influence those factors?

- WHAT are you doing to minimise the impact of negative influences?

With this insight, we can take action.

There are no magical solutions to achieving our vision – every department has its own opportunities, constraints and influencing factors that drive the process of defining and then achieving success.

However, from today, I am putting in place a programme that will enable us to take the first steps to ensure our long-term survival.

The first step is to recognise and accept that our ability to achieve our vision is dependent upon how we manage our talent and talent related activities.

The second step is to assess where we are against each of the questions I've posed to you today.

The next step is to clarify and articulate our vision, values and strategic plan.

Finally, we need to adopt a structured method of translating our vision into a set of detailed talent programmes, projects and activities that, in turn, will drive the success of the vision.

The Four Step Plan

1. Believe – we are dependent upon our people for success
2. Review – where are we today
3. Clarify – where we want to go
4. Adopt – a structured framework for all talent related activities

Over the next few weeks I will work with each of you to begin to implement the Four Step Plan. But be warned – this will be no paper exercise. What we are embarking on is a full-scale reassessment of the way we have traditionally viewed and managed our organisation. There will be a lot of heartache along the way.

We cannot leave this to chance – the future of this organisation rests on our ability to grasp this opportunity and work towards leaving a lasting legacy for all of our children.

Excerpt ends here. Any comments should be submitted personally to Her Majesty by the end of the day.

Epilogue: Some Years Later

Janus sat back in his chair and reflected on recent events. Recently promoted to his first management role, he had initially relished the opportunity to put into practice the years of learning since that fateful day when he first met the Queen.

The new job had all seemed so easy at first. He'd sought to engage his new team, presenting both the shared vision and the strategic plan that would take them there. The team had been very supportive – keen to discuss the new skills they'd need and the parts of their role that didn't support the overall plan.

Supportive, that was, until he'd set objectives that were at odds with his team's current goals.

Most had initially said they were positive, but nobody had shown any speed in getting back to him with their signatures. What with the delays and the odd little comments, he'd begun to wonder if anybody truly agreed with him.

What made it worse was that none of his team had stopped any of the activities that they all agreed were non-essential, yet they'd started to demand the training!

Where or who could he turn to in order to translate his theoretical knowledge into clear action plans?

About The Author

Guy Ellis, BA, BCom, graduated from the University of Auckland, New Zealand in 1990 and immediately moved to the United Kingdom. Initially hired by Hewlett Packard, Guy moved to the Bank of America, Citibank, and then NatWest Global Financial Markets in 1998 as Human Resources Director and Global Head of Front Office. Following the take-over of NatWest by the Royal Bank of Scotland in 2000, Guy joined Aon Limited as HR Director of its UK Consulting Division.

In 2003 Guy set up Gack Consulting to provide strategic consulting and operational support to clients implementing people based projects. Drawing upon his wide Human Resources experience, business knowledge and passion for ensuring that plans are implemented well, Guy has worked with global clients on a range of UK, EMEA and Global briefs including restructurings, resourcing models, technical and non-technical 'talent' frameworks, three year organisational plans, compensation and benefits programmes, HRIS proposals and a variety of market research activities. Guy also offers a coaching service for senior managers of selected clients.

Recognising that his clients and former business managers appreciated his straight talking style and ability to focus on key issues quickly, Guy decided to pursue a long held desire to strip away the over emphasis on technical jargon and process that characterises much 'Organisational Strategy' teaching and write a book on what he believes organisations should really be focusing on – their people. In doing so, Guy also hopes to offer a view of the future role of Human Resources – that of supporting organisational strategy through applied human psychology, legal risk analysis and expert project management skills.

Guy can be contacted at:

Gack Consulting Limited
Website: www.guyellis.net
E-mail: guy@guyellis.net
Tel: +44 (0) 7799 862 693

About The Illustrator

Caroline Evans' love of art and illustration has been with her since childhood. Now, after 25 successful years in the commercial world, she has been able to fulfill her dream of painting and illustrating full-time. Specialising in 'fairy' art, her work is currently being sold through The Circle Gallery in Berkshire. Caroline undertakes commissions and can be contacted at: caroline_evans@hotmail.co.uk

www.BookShaker.com

Your Online Haven of Wealth, Health and Happiness

Ever wondered...

How it would feel to achieve your biggest goals and dreams? Why some people seem to have it all while others struggle?

Stop wondering and start winning...

Whether you want to improve business, get better at influencing others, make your fortune or simply positively transform yourself, you'll quickly find
what you're looking for by authors who write from experience at www.BookShaker.com

Articles – Tips – Previews – Reviews

Register now at www.BookShaker.com

Plus, if it's your first visit, benefit from a 10% welcome discount when you register

Guy Ellis

If you'd like to contact Guy to...

Hire him to speak at your event

Discuss potential consulting engagements within your organisation

Consider working together or have an idea for pooling information

Interview him for your publication or media event

on the topics raised in this book and associated themes of aligning strategy and employees, the management of talent and the role of Human Resources.

Or would just like to get in touch to tell him what you think about this book.

You can call **+44 (0) 7799 862 693** or

email guy@guyellis.net

Give Tales of Talent To Your Key People So They Can Help You Achieve Your Vision

When you order Tales of Talent by the pack of 100 copies each, you qualify for a special price of just £500 per pack (a saving of £499).

Thank you.

Your Order

Please Send _____ packs (100 books) @ £500 each

subtotal _____

shipping _____

TOTAL _____

Please add shipping fee of £6.95 for every pack of 100 copies

Shipping Address

Name _____

Address_____

_____

_____

_____

Send order & cheque (made payable to Cabal Group) to:

Cabal Group (Tales of Talent)
66 Hamilton Road, Great Yarmouth
Norfolk NR30 4LZ

Printed in the United Kingdom
by Lightning Source UK Ltd.
113957UKS00001B/54